Supporting People with Problematic Behaviours - A Practice Study Guide

Pastoral Care in Criminal and Social Justice Series

www.metanoeo.weebly.com

This study guide is designed to be used with the six session training programme developed by Metanoeo. To book this training programme for your organisation please make contact via the website:

www.metanoeo.weebly.com

Introduction

Are your friends, family members or members your community involved with problematic behaviours such as addiction and offending behaviour and you find yourself wondering what you can do to help? If so, this training package has been designed for you. It will not make you an expert at helping people, but it will provide you with the opportunity to develop some fundamental knowledge and understanding, skills and approaches to help you support those you care about.

Whilst the knowledge developed through this programme is not designed to make you a substitute for professional assistance, it is important not to overlook the role that family, friends and community members can play in helping people to build a more positive life. Also, it may be that it is your intervention that sparks the first move by the individual toward the help that they need, or maintains their motivation to change when things are getting tough.

The programme is based on the fundamental beliefs that:

- Within the community there is social and human capital that can be developed to support good practice.
- All people are not only capable of change, but that a humane view of society requires a positive approach to seeing the potential people posses to flourish over just managing or intervening in their problematic behaviours.

The training programme utilises workshops with interactive team coaching and personal goal setting to help participants consider the skills, knowledge and approaches required to support people build more positive lives.

The structure of this workbook

This workbook has primarily been designed to accompany the training programme by the same name, but may be used by individuals to reflect on the topic. It aims to provoke discussion and thought on the role you might be able to play in supporting individual transformation through exploring six specific areas. These six topics have been split into three modules:

- Fundamental skills; the basics of supporting people.
- Specific behavioral focus; substance use and domestic abuse.
- Developing alternatives; thinking about promoting prosocial behaviour.

Throughout the workbook there are question breaks where you are encouraged to pause and reflect on the material you have just read and how it might be applied to your own practice within your own context. It is time for the first one now ...

Question Break 1

Consider your experiences, aspirations and expectations of engaging others in supporting change.

Individual Goals

What would you like to achieve by the end of this programme?

Module 1

Fundamental Skills

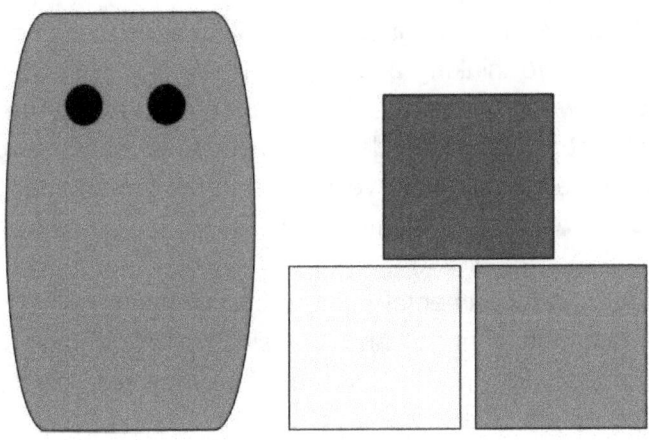

Chapter 1 - Supporting People

To be effective at supporting other people you need to be able to build relationships. People tend to change because of people and not processes. A good relationship is built on a number of features, such as:

- trust
- empathy
- honesty
- respect

It may be that these relational elements have been in your relationship for many years, or it may be that you need to develop them in a short period of time. To do this requires a genuine interest in the good of the other person and good communication skills.

When we think about communication skills it can be easy to slip into thinking about good marketing skills, but this is not what is required. If you want people to change, you cannot *sell* them the idea, you need to be able to engage with the person at a level in which they can be supported to change of their own volition.

The first fundamental point to be considered in terms of supporting change, and the skills and communication required to do this, is that it is not that you have something they want, but that the individual has something for themselves which they want to develop.

To take this perspective means recognising the importance of the individual's own perspective, and their hopes and fears. This requires the starting point of any relationship which will enable change to be based upon an understanding that their personal history and context will be influential to moving forward.

At this point it is important to recognise your role is not one of therapist or counsellor. The individual may have complex issues which require professional support and intervention. You do not need to know the details of the persons past, just a commitment to recognising each individual's history and context influences them. Your role is to help provide hope and opportunities for reconciliation which might help the person move on from their previous difficulties to develop a more fulfilling life for themselves.

Question Break 2

Think of a time when you have faced difficulties. What were the characteristics displayed by the people who helped you? What worked? What didn't?

Development of skills

Many of the skills which help people to change could be considered standard inter-personal skills. However, this does not make them something we either do or don't have. We can all develop our interpersonal skills, and in particular we will consider four:

- Communication skills
  - Verbal
  - Non-verbal
- Motivation
- Empathy
- Future focused

Communication skills take practice. Even simple things like using I instead of you statements when talking about a matter of conflict can help to diffuse defensiveness. Take some time out now to consider what you think might be beneficial with regards to the points bulleted above.

Verbal communication skills include the types of words you use, how you structure and deliver them and the perceived and intended purpose of your phrases. The use of questions (open and closed) and reflective statements are vital. However, verbal communication is strengthened or weakened by your non-verbal communication. You physical presence and presentation, appearance, body placement, furniture placement and use of gestures all contribute to the overall message.

What are the things that motivate? For each of us they may differ but understanding issues of motivation will help you to develop an effective relationship with the person with whom you are working. Whatever motivates, it has to have a future focus if intended to move people on. History helps to understand and develop empathy, but without a forward focus it will not help the person move on.

Question Break 3

What techniques can you use to create a supportive environment conducive to sharing?

Issues of which to be aware

As was highlighted above, when you develop a good relationship with someone it is likely they will share things with you which you will not be skilled to deal with. It is important in these situations to recognise your own limitations and help the person to find the right sort of support. Of course, this does not mean your role has finished, you can continue to be there, and it may be your ongoing support that keeps the person moving forward.

You may also need to guard against your relationship with the person developing in a way in which you hadn't intended. You are likely to be dealing with incredibly personal issues which can lead to a feeling of intimate knowledge of one another. Indeed, you may well have shared really personal information with the person yourself. Being clear to guard your personal safety from accusations is important.

It is also important to be aware of your expectations of each other as the relationship develops. There will be times when there is a risk of collusion or condemnation dependent upon your own personal experiences of a situation, or indeed your own mood and feelings on the day. These issues will also present themselves as your own personal 'hot spots' are touched upon. We all have issues which we continue to deal with in our own lives. It is important to think these through in terms of your relationship with the person you are helping, and how much this might influence your decisions, and how much you are comfortable to share.

As a final point remember the saying, "the more you get to know someone, the less objective your judgements about them will become".

Question Break 4

What positive techniques could you use if you wanted to support someone but started to feel out of your depth?

Individual goals

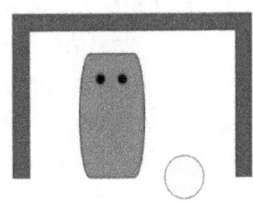

List the three things you do well, and the three things you need to improve in terms of your relational / communication skills.

Chapter 2 - Working Through the Difficult Times

No matter how great the progress an individual is making, there are likely to be points at which they will face challenges which seem impossible. At times like these the response from the individual might be:

- A sense of wanting to prove themselves
- A sense of defeat
- A sense that no matter how hard they try they cannot break the cycle
- A sense of fate

It can feel incredibly disappointing to feel that whilst you are doing everything 'right' the same issues and challenges keep coming back. As true as this is for the person grappling with an issue, it can also relate to the person trying to help them. At times like this it helps to understand the cycle of change and the importance of resilience.

When things are tough a return to old ways of acting can provide a sense of instant gratification. It can provide an initial feeling of comfort and familiarity when everything feels unfamiliar. Recognising this feeling as a need to be met instead of a failure on part of the person helps you to respond in a way which is more likely to help the individual through the difficulty. Different parts of the journey require different responses. We will start to consider these by looking at the *cycle of change*.

What challenges from your own life might it be helpful to share? When might sharing not be a good idea?

Lapse and relapse

Prochaska and DiClemente's *cycle of change* provides a helpful way of understanding the stages a person can go through in moving away from a problematic behaviour.

The *cycle of change* has six potential stages which operate in an ongoing circular pattern:

- Pre-contemplation - when an individual doesn't recognise the problem.
- Contemplation - the individual starts to become aware of the benefits of changing.
- Preparation - at this stage the individual begins to make plans to facilitate the intended change.
- Action - the person modifies the behaviour.
- Maintenance - the person has changed and is focused on maintaining that change.
- Relapse - sometimes the person can then slip right back to the beginning and need to start again.

A seventh element to the cycle could also be added, that of lapse. Lapse is more temporal than relapse. When a person experiences a lapse they continue to recognise the behaviour is unhealthy and are still committed to changing it, but may have temporarily fallen into old ways. This could be seen as a temporary move from maintenance to action.

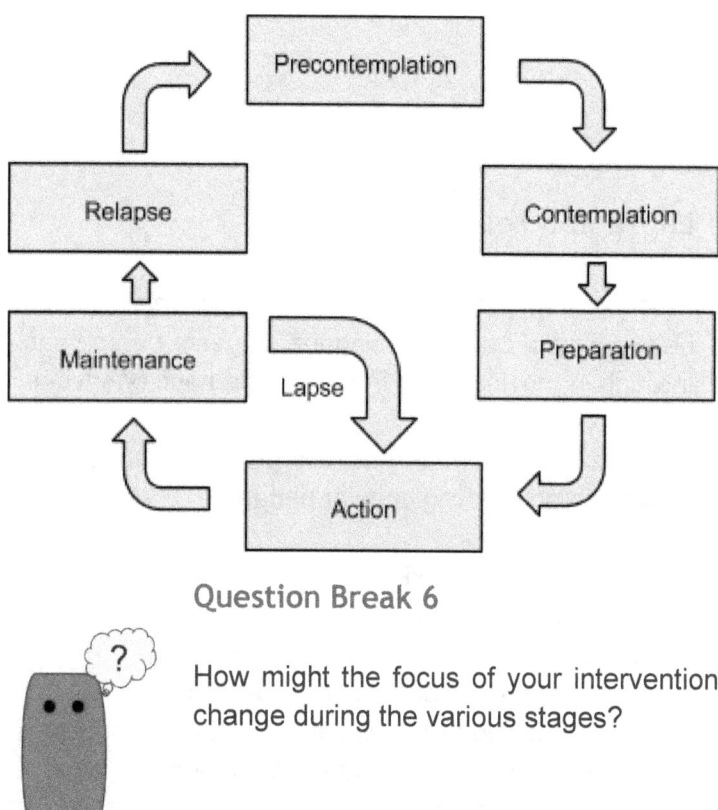

Question Break 6

How might the focus of your intervention change during the various stages?

Developing resilience

Some people seem able to discover resilience almost by their nature, but for many more, resilience can be grown through practice. Some of the techniques which might help nurture a sense of resilience include:

- Becoming confident in your strengths and abilities.
- Being optimistic and welcoming change.
- Developing and continually working on problem solving skills.
- Knowing your goals and where you want to be in life.
- Having a positive support network around you.
- Remaining aware of your own needs and asserting them.

Thinking about the last point, this can be a fine balance for any individual to achieve. It is important to remain sensitive and aware of the needs of others whilst at the same time not neglecting self.

For the practitioner there is plenty of opportunity to support the development of resilience through these concepts. For example, imagine someone who has had a history of eviction successfully telling some old friends that they will not allow them to party all night at their new property. This may provide the practitioner with an opportunity to reflect with the individual on their progress and learning.

What opportunities do you have to support the development of resilience?

Issues of which to be aware

Developing a sense of empathy and a shared relationship with an individual emphasises the commonalities between the partners in the relationship. With this in mind there is a very real danger that when the individual faces difficulties you could minimise just how difficult something might be for them, or exaggerate your own experience of something similar. It is vital to remember that this is their journey and not yours, their experience will be unique to them.

The individual you are working with may have many complicating factors which might make something which can seem straightforward to you really complex to them. Further complicating this is the idea that what might at first seem to be the issue being dealt with may not actually be the issue underpinning the behaviour.

Question Break 8

We've covered some issues which might arise. What other issues might arise which could complicate someone's change journey? How would you deal with these? What is your experience?

Individual Goals

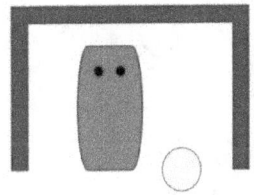

What questions do you want to incorporate into your practice in terms of helping someone to reflect on their progress?

Module 2

Specific Behavioural Focus

Chapter 3 - Dealing with Substance Use

In discussing substance use in this chapter the focus will be on the use of alcohol and illegal drugs. However, it is good to start by recognising substance use on one level could be considered as a wider issue about behaviour as opposed to legality. Addictive substances such as tobacco can also cause problems for people's health and finances but are legal. This is an important starting concept as different substances (such as many of the drugs we now consider Class A drugs such as heroin and cocaine) can become legal or illegal at different points in history. Further alcohol use in itself is not illegal. It could therefore be argued that when thinking about substance use, it is not the use that is the problem to be considered so much as the consequences. These consequences might be for the individual, their friends or family, or the wider community.

Substance use may bring problematic consequences in a number of ways:

- The impact of sustained moderate or high level use.
- The impact of binge use of a substance.
- The people the substance use brings the individual into contact with.
- The means of acquiring the substances.
- Behaviour in the lead up, during or following substance use.

Further to this the reasons or entry to use may be different and unique for each individual. For example, it is not uncommon for someone who ceases to use heroin to revert to alcohol as a means of managing problems or emotions.

Perhaps the most poignant question is to attempt to discover what the individual gets from their substance use. What is the goal? What do they gain?

Question Break 9

Is it helpful to think of substance use in a wider sense than alcohol or drug addiction? What advantages or disadvantages does this bring?

Taking positive action

There are many different approaches people use in responding to substance use. The 'cold turkey' response of withdrawing someone from a substance and locking them in a room to restore their sobriety is a popular media concept, as seen in the film *Trainspotting*. Extreme caution should be adopted with this method. **Immediate withdrawal from alcohol or drugs can result in death.** This method is therefore **not advised** as a means of responding to substance use.

Within health and criminal justice settings the health and risk approaches are popular. The health approach involves looking at the factors of substance use which may make it risky for the individual (such as sharing needles) and then intervening in these areas to keep the person safe. The risk approach seeks to address the issues which put the individual at risk of using a substance. This may include where they socialise, peers, employment, housing, emotional, physical or mental health along with a number of other factors.

Perhaps a more holistic approach would be to consider an individualised understanding and plan focusing on:

- Reasons for use
- What is missing for the person
- What is gained by use
- Danger points

This base level of understanding can then be complemented with an approach of positive psychology. This looks to grow the life the person wants and develop their strengths instead of just addressing the risk factors.

Question Break 10

Think about your own use (or lack of use) of alcohol and tobacco. What do you gain from the experience and what do you lose?

Issues of which to be aware

As highlighted, above withdrawal from substances can have extreme and severe results for an individual. Indeed, there are often numerous health factors which come into play with issues of substance use and it is therefore always recommended to ensure the person is receiving professional medical support.

The temptation for quick fixes and providing your own solutions should also be avoided. The individual needs to take the time to develop alternatives which will work for them and their reasons for using. This may be a timely and costly piece of work for the individual.

Ideas of vulnerability also need to be considered. In addition to the physical health of the individual there may also be emotional issues which may arise which were masked by the substance use. This can make them vulnerable to suggestion from others, vulnerable to themselves, but also potentially vulnerable in terms of their behaviour towards you. So along with vulnerability issues of risk also need to be considered.

Question Break 11

Have you had any positive or negative experiences of trying to help someone journeying from substance use. What have you learned from these experiences?

Individual Goals

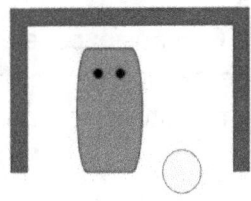

What are the issues you need to reflect on more when supporting people in their journey from substance use?

Chapter 4 - Domestic Abuse

Domestic abuse has a high level of prevalence in society. It is therefore highly likely that if you haven't experienced domestic abuse, you will be likely to know someone who has / is, although they might not have disclosed. Women's Aid have highlighted:

- One call per minute is made to the Police regarding domestic abuse.
- Two women are killed by their partner / ex-partner every week in the UK.
- 1 in 4 women and 1 in 6 men experience domestic abuse, although the experience across the genders of the level and nature of abuse differs.

Whilst attitudes are starting to change, many people still will not disclose their abuse (or perpetration) of domestic abuse. An awareness of the fundamentals is therefore of real importance, although once again, engaging professionals like Women's Support Workers is vital due to the severity of the risks involved.

A common question is why victims stay with perpetrators. The question implies a choice, but often the victim either is, or feels, powerless to choose. Further to this, leaving may have immense costs for them, their family, and often puts the person at an even greater level of risk.

What does the information around the prevalence of domestic abuse imply?

Forms of Abuse

Readers will note the use of the term domestic abuse instead of domestic violence. The reason for this use of terminology is that domestic abuse takes many forms:

- Physical
- Sexual
- Psychological
- Financial

Domestic abuse is considered to be controlled and deliberately perpetrated to achieve the aim of dominating the victim. This may be centered around controlling their behaviour, appearance, friendships, where they go, what they do or how they spend their money.

Physical abuse may be perpetrated in many forms. A common feature of which to be aware is bruises being in areas which other people will not see. Again, this is reflective of the idea that domestic abuse is not so much perpetrated in a fit of rage as it is in a planned and controlled manner.

Domestic abuse may also be sexual in it's nature. For example, unwanted sexual advances, rape, demanding sexual acts which the victim does not want to engage in and unwanted sexualisation of conversations.

Abuse may be present in a psychological form through put downs and the victim being made to question themselves and what they do. Friendships and the influence of family members may be questioned and demands made on who the victim see's, where they go and what they wear.

Finances may also be controlled in various ways to ensure the victim does not have access or control over their own money. This is an important factor as money can provide a form of independence.

Question Break 13

What are the implications of considering domestic *abuse* instead of domestic *violence* for helping people?

Working with perpetrators

It is vital that victims, and perpetrators, are offered professional support due to the severe nature of the potential for harm. However, this does not discount the role of friends and family. Indeed, this informal support, based on awareness of the factors around domestic abuse, can help to maintain an awareness for the victim or perpetrator that the abuse is not acceptable. You can provide a vital role in preventing normalisation and acceptance of abusive behaviours.

It is vital to consider the victim's safety in all you do. Think about what you disclose when talking and what impact this might have on the victim. Conversations need to be considered and informed by an awareness of the potential consequences for the victim. It is also important to consider the impact for any children present who may witness or simply be aware of the abuse. Research has shown there is a significant impact on children who witness domestic abuse between adults.

It is important not provide a false sense of hope. There are likely to be many times when a perpetrator will promise never to act the same way again, this may be a genuine promise or a means of maintaining control when someone is about to leave. However, it is unlikely that there will be any 'miracle cure' changes to behaviours which for the perpetrator have proved successful in the past.

Another factor to consider is that of the correlation of external factors such as substance use, loss of employment, bereavement and a host of other potential stressors. Whilst these factors do not explain or excuse the abusive behaviour they may increase the risk of it occurring.

There are many forms of interventions available. Again, it is important that professional support is engaged. However, on a more positive side it is important for the victim and abuser to develop their knowledge and expectations of what healthy relationships look like. This may be a very alien expectation as victims and perpetrators alike may never have experienced any concept of what a healthy relationship may comprise.

One final issue of which to be aware is that of personalisation. Be aware that when supporting people through issues of domestic abuse it is very easy to start to misread matters into other areas of your own life.

Question Break 14

What are the indicators which would trigger a call to:
- the Police?
- Social Services?
- the person's partner?

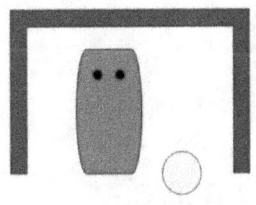

Individual Goals

Domestic abuse is an emotionally difficult subject. Consider how you can protect yourself physically and emotionally in this area.

Module 3

Developing Alternatives

Chapter 5 - Promoting Pro-Social Behaviour 1

It is helpful to think of change as an ongoing journey rather than a one off decision. The concept of a journey can be quite collaborative and can encourage the idea of journeying together to find change and the life that is desired. Within the concept of change as a journey, the person changing sets the direction and speed of travel. There will be times when they will need to rest, times when they will face obstacles and distractions, and times when they are travelling without difficulty. Your role is as a journeying companion.

As a journeying companion you can help the individual to reflect on what sort of future they would like and how they can achieve their desire. You can help the person to reflect on what skills they have and what they need to develop. You can help them look at their social networks to see what impact this has, and also the consequences of their decisions for those they care about (more about this in the final chapter).

Many professionals will have a requirement to consider the 'risk factors' for the individual; what might increase the possibility of unhealthy or dangerous behaviours. However, in a less formal role you can be free to concentrate on the development of potential instead of management of risk. You can help the individual to explore their vision and values and understand what makes them unique and individual. Part of your role will be to help the individual discover their strengths and areas for development.

Question Break 15

What are the pro's and con's of developing alternative behaviours and thoughts as an approach?

Internal factors

In considering the internal factors which will influence the change journey you will be considering a number of factors:

- Self-esteem
- Knowledge
- Patience
- Attitude
- Confidence
- Understanding
- Emotional intelligence
- Beliefs

These are areas which we all work on throughout our lives. This can be helpful as it can facilitate a genuine sharing of experiences and joint journeying. A key idea here is exploring the concepts, not judging or proposing your ideals. Areas such as the eight above will define how the person experiences their life and their world.

Question Break 16

What practical things could you do to develop each of the eight factors identified? What other factors could you add?

External factors

We will now highlight eight external factors which can be considered crucial to the change journey:

- Accommodation
- Substance use
- Peer groups
- Relationships
- Employment, Training and Education
- Health and wellbeing
- Membership of formal or informal groups
- Hobbies and interests

Again, the key is to understand where the individual is in relation to these issues. Something that might seem important to you might not be important to them. Something which you might see as a strength or as problematic might not be perceived in the same way by the individual. Ask them for their views, listen to their experiences and desires. Finally, remember, you cannot offer solutions to all the problems, be prepared to help the person find the appropriate support and to be realistic in their desired outcomes.

Question Break 17

What practical things could you do to develop each of the eight factors identified? What other factors could you add?

Individual Goals

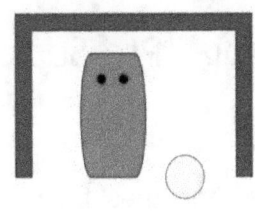

Each of the 16 factors identified could act as a positive or a negative. How could you test the influence of each of these in your practice?

Chapter 6 - Promoting Pro-Social Behaviour 2

Over the past couple of decades there has been an increase in cognitive behavioural approaches to dealing with offending behaviour. In this final chapter we will consider some simple exercises which can be used from the field of cognitive behavioural theory to help develop your discussions with the people with whom you might be working.

Before we move on to some exercises it is important to contextualise cognitive behavioural techniques. Whilst there might appear to be an emphasis on problem solving skills and techniques, this should compliment the personal and social factors discussed in the previous chapter. Developing good problem solving will not take away the influence of the factors previously considered.

Question Break 18

You will now be introduced to a number of exercises. How could you use these exercises for a situation in your own life?

A-B-C analysis

This involves exploring the build up to the behaviour and the consequences. It is intended to help the individual learn from exploring and analysing the situation.

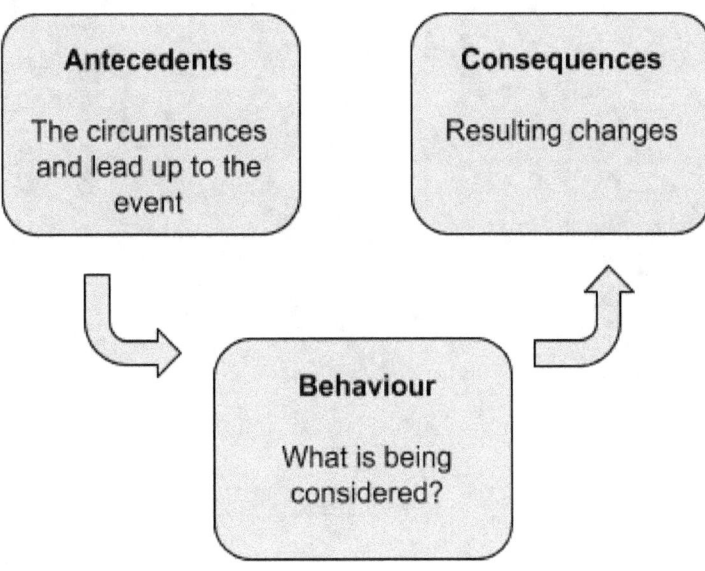

Making choices

These exercises are centred around providing the individual with a basic framework for making decisions.

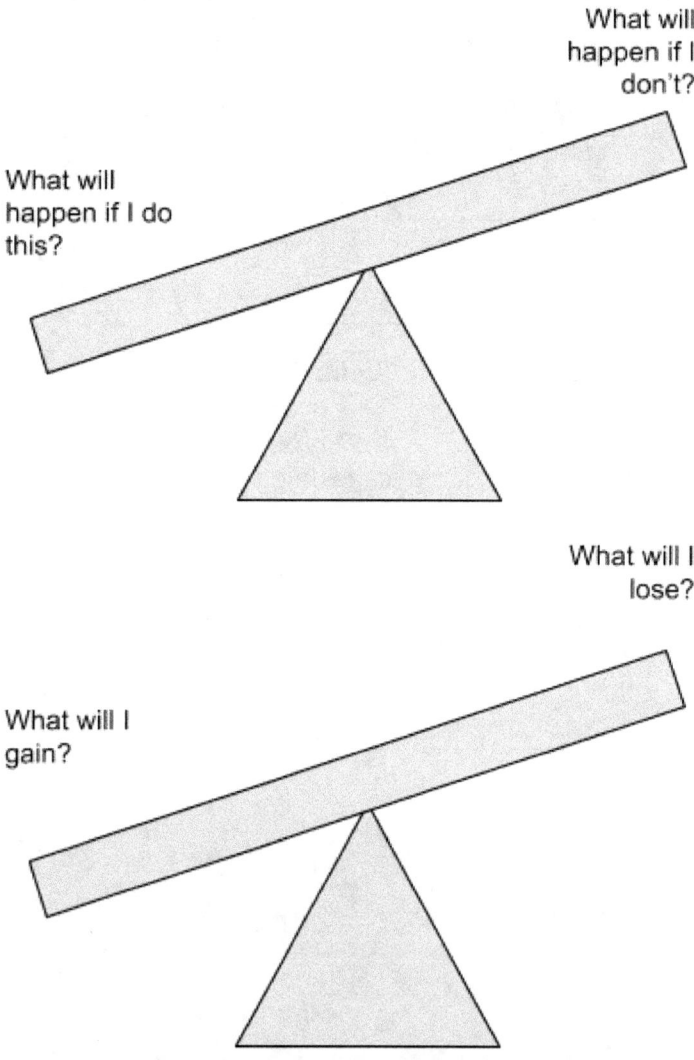

Considering understanding

This exercise is designed to evoke discussion around the beliefs the individual has which underpin their decision making.

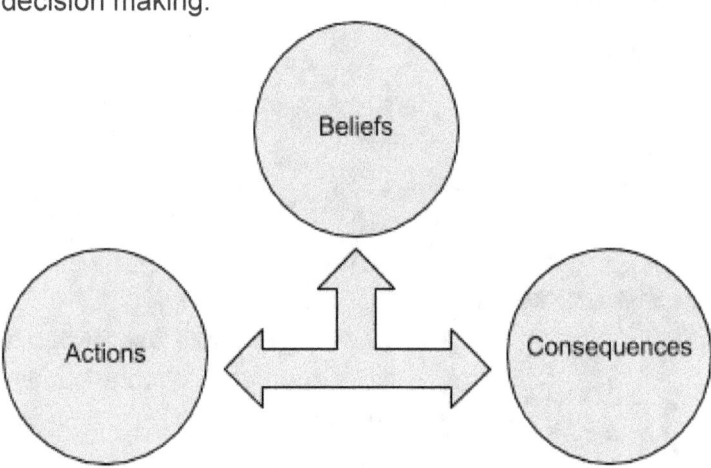

It can be useful to compliment this exercise by looking at what the individual considers their needs to be and how they attempt to meet these.

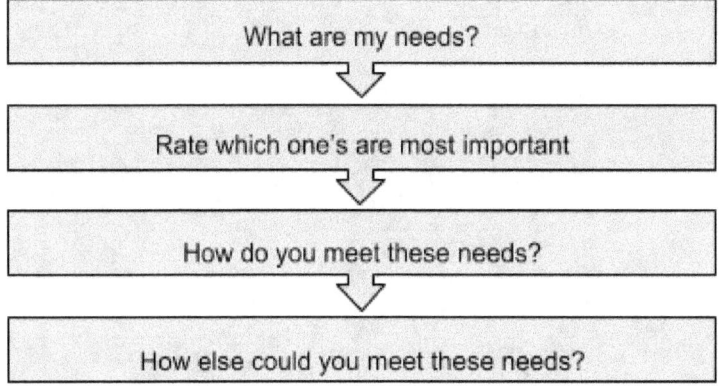

Question Break 19

What have you learned from the exercises?

Individual Goals

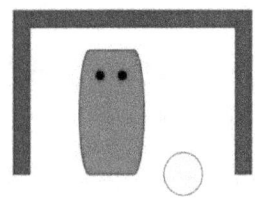

How could I make use of thinking skills approaches more subtly in what I do?

Conclusion

This short course on supporting those at risk of problematic behaviours has covered some of the basics in terms of skills, understanding and practice.

We all can play a role in supporting people in their change journey. A good place to start after completion of this course would be to build your awareness of the support services which are available in your area.

Remember, change takes time, and it also requires a sense of hope. This is not the same as complacency or ignorance of any factors of risk, but at the base level we all need people who will care for us and believe in us. Don't underestimate the role you can play in supporting those you care about to build a more positive life!

Question Break 20

Reviewing the material covered:

List 3 positives approaches you can take.
List 3 dangers of which to be aware.

Individual Goals

Throughout this study guide you have been encouraged to set yourself specific goals in relation to your own approach to faith and practice. The final goal will now be set along with an encouragement to review your preceding goals.

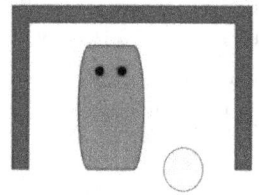

What more do you need to learn to increase the effectiveness of the support you can offer to other people?

Introduction goal completed:

Chapter 1 goal completed:

Chapter 2 goal completed:

Chapter 3 goal completed:

Chapter 4 goal completed:

Chapter 5 goal completed:

Chapter 6 goal completed:

Conclusion goal completed:

About Metanoeo

Metanoeo is a social enterprise engaging faith in the journey from problematic behaviours (including addiction, antisocial behaviour 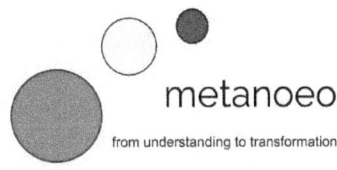 and crime) in practice, the community and academia. In addition to training, *Metanoeo* offers consultancy and research services and academic courses and programmes. *Metanoeo* offers those with difficult behaviours the opportunity to engage in a life coaching scheme to help them use their faith or openness to faith build a positive identity and lifestyle.

About the author

Dave has thirteen years experience as a probation practitioner and manager helping to rehabilitate those convicted of crime. He has also lectured and published in  criminal and community justice and is presently completing his PhD in Theology and Criminology. Dave established *Metanoeo* in 2014.